Making Their Mark: Women in Science and Medicine™

Elizabeth Blackwell
The First Woman Doctor

Liza N. Burby

The Rosen Publishing Group's
PowerKids Press™
New York

Published in 1997 by The Rosen Publishing Group, Inc.
29 East 21st Street, New York, NY 10010

First Edition

Book Design: Erin McKenna

Photo Credits: Cover and pp. 4, 8, 12, 16, 19, 20 © Corbis-Bettmann; p. 7, 11, 15 © Corbis Bettmann.

Burby, Liza N.
    Elizabeth Blackwell / by Liza N. Burby
        p.   cm. — (Making their mark)
    Includes index.
    Summary: A simple presentation of the achievements of the woman who was the first to enter medical school, who established the first nursing school in the United States, who began medical colleges for women, and who made it possible for other women to become doctors.
    ISBN 0-8239-5022-0 (library bound)
    1. Blackwell, Elizabeth, 1901-1978—Juvenile literature. 2. Women physicians—United States—Biography—Juvenile literature. 3. Women physicians—England—Biography—Juvenile literature. [1. Blackwell, Elizabeth, 1821–1910. 2. Physicians. 3. Women—Biography.] I. Title. II. Series: Burby, Liza N. Making their mark.
R154.B623B87 1996
610' .92—dc20   96–41732
[B]   CIP
                                                      AC

Manufactured in the United States of America

Contents

Equal Education

Elizabeth Blackwell was born in England on February 3, 1821. In those days, girls were expected to marry and become mothers. Elizabeth's father, Samuel, believed that his sons and daughters should receive the same education. Elizabeth learned subjects such as math and science. Most girls only learned music and sewing. Elizabeth wanted to do something no woman had ever done before.

◀ Elizabeth was able to study the same subjects as her brothers in school.

5

The Blackwells Move to America

When Elizabeth was eleven, her father's successful sugar factory burned down. Samuel had always wanted to go to the United States. He decided that the fire was a sign that his family should leave England. So the Blackwells moved to New York. Samuel's sugar business did not do very well there. The family moved around a lot. When Elizabeth was seventeen, they settled in Cincinnati, Ohio. A few weeks after they moved there, her father died.

In the 1800s, many people came to the United States from other countries. ▶

Elizabeth Becomes a Teacher

The Blackwells had very little money left. So Elizabeth's mother, Hannah, and her three daughters turned their home into a girls' school. Elizabeth did not really like teaching, but she helped her family until she was 24 years old. Within a few years, her brothers, Samuel and Henry, were able to earn enough money as traveling salesmen to support the family. But Elizabeth was **restless** (REST-less). She had a dream to do something special.

◀ Although Elizabeth worked at her family's school, she wanted to do something different.

9

A Dream Begins

One day Elizabeth visited a friend who was very sick. The woman said that Elizabeth should become a doctor. At first Elizabeth thought this was funny. She knew that no woman had ever been allowed to go to medical school. But this challenge excited her. Now she knew what she would do with her life. She would become the first woman doctor!

No woman had ever been allowed to go to medical school. Elizabeth decided to change that. ▶

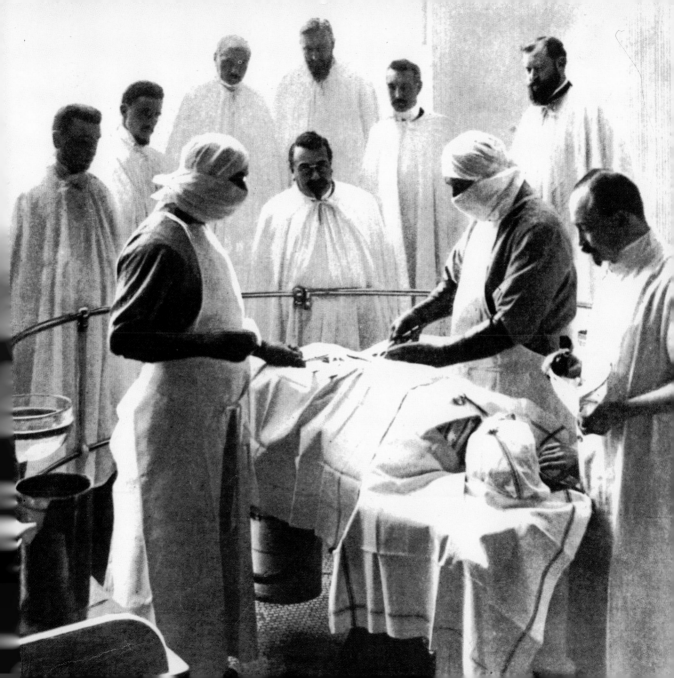

Preparing for Medical School

Elizabeth knew she would have to earn money to pay for medical school. She became a teacher in North Carolina. When she wasn't working, she studied books about medicine so she would be ready for medical school. In 1847, she went to Philadelphia to study **anatomy** (ah-NA-tom-ee). This made Elizabeth very excited about going to medical school.

◀ Elizabeth paid for her medical school by working as a teacher.

13

Refused by the Best Schools

Elizabeth applied to all of the best medical schools in the United States. Each school told her that women could only be nurses. One doctor suggested that she pretend to be a man to get into medical school. This idea made Elizabeth angry. "I want to go as a woman!" she said. "Or what good will I be to the women who follow?"

Elizabeth was told the only way she could ▶ work in medicine was as a nurse.

Accepted as a Joke

Elizabeth was **discouraged** (dih-SKUR-ijd). Then Geneva Medical College in New York accepted her. Elizabeth found out later that she was accepted as a joke. The students had voted to let her come, but they thought she would be too ashamed to do it. But Elizabeth was **dedicated** (DED-ih-kay-ted) to **medicine** (MED-ih-sin). She earned the **respect** (ree-SPEKT) of her teachers and the students. Two years later, she finished as one of the best students in the class.

◀ In Elizabeth's time, women needed a special dedication to study medicine and finish medical school.

An Accident Spoils a Dream

On January 23, 1849, Elizabeth Blackwell became a doctor. But no hospital in the United States would let her work. She went to Paris, France, where she became a nurse in a hospital. She watched the doctors carefully. She decided to be a **surgeon** (SER-jun). But this dream was spoiled when she accidentally squirted a strong medicine in her eyes. She was very sick for a long time and lost sight in her left eye. She moved back home to get better.

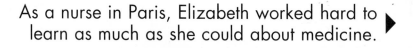
As a nurse in Paris, Elizabeth worked hard to learn as much as she could about medicine. ▶

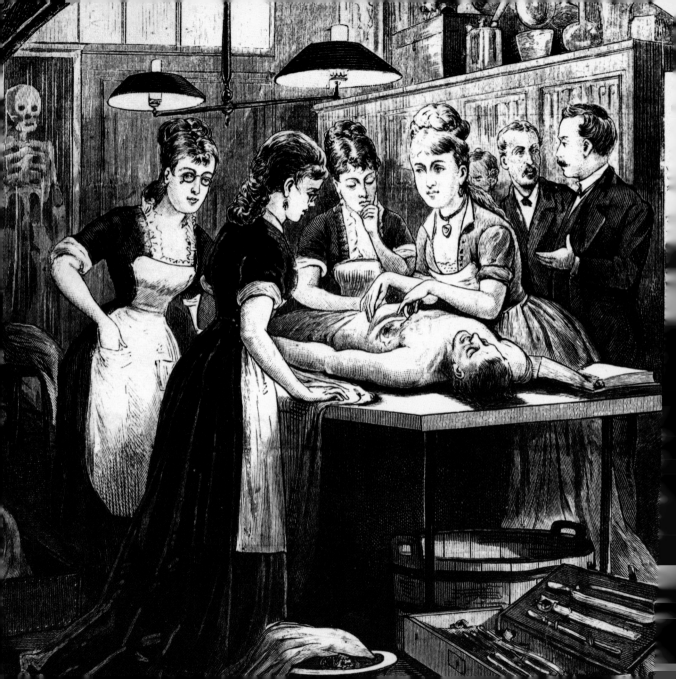

A Hospital of Her Own

Elizabeth became a very good doctor. In 1852, she opened her own office in New York City. Five years later, she and her younger sister, Emily, opened a hospital called the New York **Infirmary** (in-FIRM-ah-REE) for Women and Children. The hospital had the first nursing school in the United States. Many sick people were helped by the important work of the doctors and nurses at Elizabeth's hospital.

◄ Elizabeth's hard work made it possible for other women to study medicine and become doctors.

A Dream Comes True

Elizabeth Blackwell wanted other women to become doctors, too. In 1866, she opened a medical college for women in New York City. Later, she helped to open another college in England. Elizabeth Blackwell died in 1910. By that time, women were going to medical school. Her dream to do something that no woman had done before had helped other women. Elizabeth had changed medicine forever.

Glossary

anatomy (ah-NA-tom-ee) The study of the human body.

dedicate (DED-ih-kayt) To work hard for a belief.

discourage (dih-SKUR-ij) To feel like giving up.

infirmary (in-FIRM-ah-REE) A place where the sick and hurt are cared for.

medicine (MED-ih-sin) The science of making sick people well and keeping them healthy.

respect (ree-SPEKT) To admire someone.

restless (REST-less) Unable to sit still.

surgeon (SER-jun) A person who operates on sick people.

Index